Professor G. Steward's directions to the *Which is Best Test*.

The *Which is Best Test* is designed to test your decision making skills. There are three multiple choice questions were you will be able to guess which is best. Professor G. Steward's formula will determine which answer is correct. His formula is **Success+Goal-Time-Stress=Best**.

My name is Jimmy. I like to make good decisions but I hate to guess. My mother always told me not to be afraid to ask for help. Can you help me with a simple test? Can you help me decide which is best?

Question 1

1) Jimmy wants a bike. He desires to ride with his friends this week. His parents gave him three options. Let's help Jimmy chose which is best.

   A) Jimmy's parents can afford to buy him a used bike. The used bike has many problems but Jimmy can afford to purchase it without waiting until a later date.

   B) Jimmy's parents can buy him the bike of his dreams but he has to wait two weeks before they can afford it.

   C) Jimmy can get a new game for his computer instead of getting a bike. He can share a bike with his friend but he will be limited to how often he gets to ride.

Your answer _____

Question 1

Explain why you chose this answer._____

_____

_____

_____

_____

_____

Which answer did you guess? Let's see which is best!

Formula for determining BEST!

Success +Goal-Time-Stress

Question 1) *A) Jimmy's parents can afford to buy him a used bike. The used bike has many problems but Jimmy can afford to purchase it without waiting to a later date.*

<u>Success</u> – Does Jimmy get to ride a bike?

Yes, but he takes the chance of the bike breaking down because it is a used bike.

Professor G Steward rewards **7 Points**

<u>**Goal**</u>- Does Jimmy set a high goal?

No, Jimmy settles for a used bike with known problems.

Question 1 Answer A

Professor G Steward rewards **3 Points**

<u>Time</u>- Does Jimmy achieve his goal in a timely fashion?

   Yes, Jimmy gets to ride a bike immediately.

Professor G Steward rewards **0 Points**

<u>Stress</u>- Does Jimmy create future problems for his self?

   Yes, Jimmy will have to repair his bike because it is used and has problems.

Professor G Steward rewards **8 Points**

       Success +Goal-Time-Stress

7+3-0-8= _____

Question 1) *B) Jimmy's parents can buy him the bike of his dreams but he has to wait two weeks before they can afford it.*

Success – Does Jimmy get to ride a bike?

Yes, but Jimmy has to wait two weeks before he can ride his bike.

*Professor G Steward rewards **4 Points***

Goal - Does Jimmy set a high goal?

Yes, Jimmy waits and receives a brand new bike of his dreams.

*Professor G Steward rewards **10 Points***

Time - Does Jimmy achieve his goal in a timely fashion?

Yes, Jimmy will be able to ride his bike in two weeks but does not get to ride a bike immediately.

Question 1 Answer B

Professor G Steward rewards **5 Points**

Stress- Does Jimmy create future problems for himself?

No, Jimmy sacrificed riding his bike for two weeks and now he can ride his bike without any issues.

Professor G Steward rewards **0 Points**

       Success +Goal-Time-Stress

4+10-5-0=_____

Question 1) C) *Jimmy can get a new game for his computer instead of getting a bike. He can share a bike with his friend but he will be limited to how often he gets to ride.*

Success – Does Jimmy get to ride a bike?

Yes, Jimmy gets to ride his friend's bike but he will be limited to how much time he gets to ride. He can only ride the bike when his friend allows him to.

*Professor G Steward rewards **5 Points***

Goal- Does Jimmy set a high goal?

No, Jimmy wants his own bike but he settles for sharing a bike with a friend. Jimmy also gets a game for his computer which will entertain him but will not satisfy his desire to ride a bike.

*Professor G Steward rewards **4 Points***

Question 1 Answer C

Time - Does Jimmy achieve his goal in a timely fashion?

No, Jimmy gets to ride his friend's bike immediately but he still will have no bike of his own.

Professor G Steward rewards **4 Points**

Stress - Does Jimmy create future problems for himself?

Yes, Jimmy will soon have to buy his own bike. He will not want to continue sharing a bike with his friend.

Professor G Steward rewards **5 Points**

Success +Goal-Time-Stress

5+4-4-5=_____

Professor G Steward question # 1 **correct answer.** *B) Jimmy's parents can buy him the bike of his dreams but he has to wait two weeks before they can afford it.*

A) 7+3-0-8= **2 Points**

B) 4+10-5-0= **9 Points**

C) 5+4-4-5= **0 Points**

Question 2

Can you help me with a simple test? Can you help me decide which is best?

Question 2) Jimmy wants to go to his best friend's party Saturday but he has a big homework assignment due Monday. Let's help Jimmy with a simple test. Let's help Jimmy decide which is best.

    A) Jimmy should go home Friday after school and immediately finish all of his homework. Jimmy won't be able to go outside and play at all Friday. Jimmy will be able to go to his friend's party Saturday and he will be free to go outside Sunday.

    B) Jimmy should put off his homework until Sunday. He can go outside on Friday after school and go to his friend's party Saturday.

C) Jimmy should start his homework Friday but finish it Sunday. This way he can go outside Friday and still make it to his friend's party Saturday.

Your answer _____

Question 2

Explain why you chose this answer._____

_____

_____

_____

_____

_____

Which answer did you guess? Let's see which is best!

Formula for determining BEST!

Success +Goal-Time-Stress

Question 2) *A) Jimmy should go home Friday after school and immediately finish all of his homework. Jimmy won't be able to go outside and play at all Friday. Jimmy will be able to go to his friend party Saturday and he will be free to go outside and play Sunday.*

<u>Success</u> – Does Jimmy get to go to his friend's party and avoid not completing the homework assignment?

Yes, Jimmy will be able to go to his friend's party. He also will finish his homework before going to the party. This will prevent Jimmy for worrying about his work the entire weekend.

Professor G Steward rewards **10 Points**

<u>**Goal**</u>- Does Jimmy set a high goal?

Yes, Jimmy makes sure he finishes his homework first because it is the most important thing he needs to do. He also is able to do what he wants to do which is attend his friend's party because he already has completed his work.

Professor G Steward rewards **10 Points**

<u>**Time**</u>- Does Jimmy achieve his goal in a timely fashion?

Yes, Jimmy finishes homework as soon as he gets home. He does not wait until the last moment. Jimmy is able to go to his friend's party Saturday as well.

Question 2 Answer A

Professor G Steward rewards 0 Points

Stress- Does Jimmy create future problems for himself?

No, Jimmy has nothing to worry about because his work will be done before he goes to party.

Professor G Steward rewards **0 Points**

Success +Goal-Time-Stress

10+10-0-0=_____

Question 2) B) *Jimmy should put off his homework until Sunday. He can go outside on Friday after school and go to his friend's party Saturday.*

<u>Success</u> – Does Jimmy get to go to his friend's party and avoid not completing the homework assignment?

Yes, Jimmy gets to go to his friend's party but Jimmy waits until the last minute to finish his homework. This may cause Jimmy to rush and not do as well as he should.

Professor G Steward rewards **5 Points**

<u>**Goal**</u>- Does Jimmy set a high goal?

No, Jimmy does not handle his main concern first. Jimmy is more concerned with having fun at his friend's party than taking care of what's most important.

*Professor G Steward rewards **3 Points***

<u>Time</u>- Does Jimmy achieve his goal in a timely fashion?

    No, Jimmy puts off his homework until the last minute leaving room for mistakes. He does not take into account that other things may happen between Friday and Sunday that may keep him from completing his work if he waits.

*Professor G Steward rewards **8 Points***

<u>Stress</u>- Does Jimmy create future problems for himself?

    Yes, Jimmy waits to finish homework forcing himself to rush to complete it Sunday. If Jimmy has any problems with the homework he will not have time to get the best help he would desire.

Question 2 Answer B

Professor G Steward rewards **8 Points**

Success +Goal-Time-Stress

5+3-8-8=_____

Question 2) C) *Jimmy should start his homework Friday but finish it Sunday. This way he can go outside Friday and still make it to his friend's party Saturday.*

Success – Does Jimmy get to go to his friend's party and avoid not completing the homework assignment?

Yes, Jimmy gets to go to his friend's party. He starts his homework Friday and finishes it Sunday. It is good that he works on his homework Friday. It may cause problems to wait to finish his homework Sunday right before the assignment is due.

Professor G Steward rewards **7 Points**

Goal- Does Jimmy set a high goal?

Yes, Jimmy starts his homework on Friday because he knows it is important for him to do well on this assignment. Jimmy also is able to attend his friend's party. Jimmy waits to complete his homework on Sunday which may cause Jimmy to not put as much effort into it as he should. Jimmy will have to rush to complete the homework because it is due the next day.

Professor G Steward rewards **6 Points**

<u>*Time*</u>- Does Jimmy achieve his goal in a timely fashion?

    No, Jimmy does not complete his homework until Sunday. He starts his work Friday but waits until the last minute to finish it on Sunday. Jimmy does well by getting some of the homework complete early but still leaves room for error by waiting until Sunday to complete the assignment.

Question 2 Answer C

Professor G Stewart rewards **4 Points**

<u>Stress</u>- Does Jimmy create future problems for himself?

Yes, by not completing his homework as soon as he could, Jimmy is now forced to rush to finish his work.

Professor G Stewart rewards **4 Points**

Success +Goal-Time-Stress

7+6-4-4=_____

Professor G Stewart question # **2 correct answer.** *A) Jimmy should go home Friday after school and immediately finish all of his homework. Jimmy won't be able to go outside and play at all Friday. Jimmy will be able to go to his friend's party Saturday and he will be free to go outside Sunday.*

A)10+10-0-0= *20 Points*

B)5+3-8-8= *-8 Points*

C)7+6-4-4= *5 Points*

Can you help me with a simple test? Can you help me decide which is best?

Question 3) Jimmy is great at math but not as good with writing. Jimmy's teacher is having career day and the students must choose which career they want to research. Let's help Jimmy with a little test. Let's help Jimmy decide which is best.

 A) Jimmy should choose to research becoming an author at career day, this way he can learn more about writing.

 B) Jimmy should choose to research becoming an art teacher at career day because he thinks it would be a fun experience.

C) Jimmy should research becoming an accountant at career day. He is already great at math and this could help him be prepared when the time comes to decide his future job.

Your answer _____

Question 3

Explain why you chose this answer._____

_____

_____

_____

_____

_____

Which answer did you guess? Let's see which is best!

Formula for determining BEST!

Success +Goal-Time-Stress

Question 3) A) *Jimmy should choose to research becoming an author at career day, this way he can learn more about writing.*

<u>Success</u> – Does Jimmy research a career that is similar to his skill set and could be useful for his career search in the future?

No, Jimmy chooses to research writing because he is not very good at it. He has good motives but career day is the wrong setting. Career day is to help you match your skill set with a career you would enjoy in the future.

Professor G Steward rewards **5 Points**

Goal- Does Jimmy set a high goal?

Yes, Jimmy wants to improve his writing which is good but Jimmy does not take advantage of the purpose of the career day.

Professor G Steward rewards **5 Points**

Time- Does Jimmy use his time wisely?

No, Jimmy attempts to learn useful information but career days are not used to show you how to do the career. Career days help you decide if you would like to do the career in the future.

Professor G Steward rewards **4 Points**

Stress- Does Jimmy create future problems for himself?

Yes, Jimmy may not enjoy learning about being an author since he does not like writing. Jimmy may regret not learning about a career he would have been more interested in.

Professor G Steward rewards **6 Points**

Success +Goal-Time-Stress

5+5-4-6=_____

Question 3) *B) Jimmy should choose to research becoming an art teacher at career day because he thinks it would be a fun experience.*

Success -Does Jimmy research a career that is similar to his skill set and could be useful for his career search in the future?

No, Jimmy chooses a career that he has no intent to follow up on. Jimmy only chooses this career because he thinks it would be fun.

Professor G Steward rewards **0 Points**

Goal- Does Jimmy set a high goal?

No, Jimmy did not take the career day serious. Jimmy's only concern was having a good time.

Question 3 Answer B

*Professor G Steward rewards **0 Points***

Time- Does Jimmy use his time wisely?

No, Jimmy does not achieve any goal that will be beneficial in the future.

*Professor G Steward rewards **10 Points***

Stress- Does Jimmy create future problems for himself?

Yes, Jimmy does not get any information that will help him use his skills in the future.

*Professor G Steward rewards **10 Points***

Success +Goal-Time-Stress

0+0-10-10=_____

Question 3) C) *Jimmy should research becoming an accountant at career day. He is already great at math and this could help him be prepared when the time comes to decide his future job.*

Success -Does Jimmy research a career that is similar to his skill set and could be useful for his career search in the future?

Yes, Jimmy chooses to research becoming an accountant. Jimmy is great at math and an accountant is a job that meanly deals with math. Jimmy could possibly do this job in the future.

Professor G Steward rewards **10 Points**

Goal- Does Jimmy set a high goal?

Yes, Jimmy chooses to research a career that fits his skill set and will be a good career for him if he continues to enjoy math.

Professor G Steward rewards **10 Points**

Time- Does Jimmy use his time wisely?

Yes, Jimmy chooses to research a career that he may go into. Jimmy's time is being used productively learning about the good his math talent may bring.

Professor G Steward rewards **0 Points**

Stress- Does Jimmy create future problems for himself?

No, Jimmy is thinking about the future with this choice. Jimmy gives himself a head start on his future in deciding what he will want to do.

Professor G Steward rewards **0 Points**

Success +Goal-Time-Stress

10+10-0-0=_____

Professor G Stewart question # **3 correct answer. C)** *Jimmy should research becoming an accountant at career day. He is already great at math and this could help him be prepared when the time comes to decide his future job.*

A)5+5-4-6= **0 Points**

B)0+0-10-10= **-20 Points**

C)10+10-0-0= **20 Points**

It's great to have friends who are so smart. Thanks so much with all my heart. I will never be afraid to ask for help. With your help I am ready for any test. Thanks for helping me decide which is best!

Made in the USA
Columbia, SC
03 December 2021